SEEING THE LIGHT

SEEING THE LIGHT

JAMES BROUGHTON

CITY LIGHTS

2nd printing: July 1978

Portions of this book have been printed previously in *Untitled*, *Film Culture*, *Filmmakers Newsletter* and *Canyon Cinemanews*.

"The Brotherhood of Light" is reproduced by permission of the Friends of Photography from their journal, *Untitled*, no. 7/8.

Library of Congress Cataloging in Publication Data

Broughton, James Richard, 1913–
   Seeing the light.

   Bibliography p: 80
   1. Moving-pictures—Philosophy. 2. Moving-pictures—Production and direction. I. Title.
PN1995.B74   791.43'01   76-30681
ISBN 0-87286-090-6

CITY LIGHTS BOOKS are published at the City Lights Bookstore, Broadway & Columbus, San Francisco, California 94133.

For my students, my peers, and my gods

Table of Contents

PHOTOGRAPHS:

Cover James Broughton (by Joel Singer)
p. 9 James Broughton filming *Testament*, 1974
      (by Robert A. Haller)
p. 10 *Dreamwood*, 1972
p. 35 *Mother's Day*, 1948
p. 36 *The Pleasure Garden*, 1953
p. 37 *The Bed*, 1968
p. 38 *The Golden Positions*, 1970
p. 77 *Erogeny*, 1976
p. 78 *Testament*, 1974

Coming into Focus

When I was 30 my greatest consolation was the thought of suicide. But that was three years before I began to make films. What a lot of vicissitude, ecstasy and ennui I would have missed!

Did the creation of moving black and white images save my life? It is certain that I have never seriously contemplated suicide since. 'It takes a long time to become young,' said Picasso.

*

Of techniques of film there are many manuals.

Of critiques there are innumerable opinions.

Of illuminations there are only fitful flashes.

I for one could wish for more perception of the poetic view. For me cinema is not social phenomenon or cultural question mark, it is a potential oracle of the imagination. For me cinema is poetry and love and religion and my duty to the Lords of Creation. I use these terms interchangeably.

*

I am not talking here about going to the movies. I am talking about making cinema. I am talking about the life of vision. I am talking about cinema as one way of living the life of a poet. I am talking about film as poetry, as philosophy, as metaphysics, as all else it has not yet dared to become.

Einstein said: 'The most beautiful thing we can experience is the mysterious. It is the source of all true art and science.'

*

Going to the movies, to indulge your fantasies or to have critical opinions, is certainly one way to pass your time. But it has little to do with the art of bringing the movie to life or bringing life to the movie. Be wary: life is what happens while you are doing something else.

*

'Try, as if you were one of the first men, to say what you see and experience and love and lose,' wrote Rilke to his questioning young poet. Only thus will you discover what Emerson called your own peculiar 'angle to the universe.'

True poets are as anarchic as Jesus and Lao-Tzu. They particularly love revolutions, for revolutions are symbols of freedom from the major enemies of art: cops, critics, and collective inertia.

Every artist is in revolt. Because he is revolted by the passion for ignorance, greed and laziness in his fellow men. He knows a livelier realm where they might dwell, if only they could see the Light. So he tries to show them the Light. And they can't see it. They don't want to see it. They say, 'I don't see anything in it.' So he tries again. He lights another lamp, he makes another revolution.

But let us keep clear what kind of revolution we are talking about.

Poets are not moral examples to society. Their value is in being obstreperous, outlandish and obscene. Their business is to ignite a revolution of insight in the soul.

*

Analytical theorizing is often felt to be 'over one's head.' It is nothing of the sort. It is actually under one's feet. It is the mud one has to wade through: the bog of literal minds who build labyrinthine swamps of intellect to preserve themselves from direct experience. What is truly over one's head is the realm of the poetic imagination. As Barnett Newman put it: 'Aesthetics is for the artist as ornithology is for the birds.'

*

So look up and look out and seek the Light that flies.

When you travel, don't follow the main roads. Get lost.

If you are too choosey about the spaces you visit, you may miss Inspiration Point.

*

Cinema like life is only worth living when it is in the service of something beyond the explicit and the mundane.

When Marianne Moore was asked whether she wrote poetry for fame or for money, she replied, 'Are there no other alternatives?'

Some years ago I came upon the following sentence (author unknown to me): 'The purpose of life is to discover what the Glory of

13

God is, and then to spend your life celebrating it.' This banal sentence has kept me busy ever since. Such a view is not at all in fashion: nowadays we are encouraged to view the Glory of God as a problem or a despair. Secretly poets know better. However much they may grumble, they are enchanted by what they discover, shape and reveal.

We may not be able to alter our births and deaths, but we can render the interval between them more endurable. And even transcendent. 'Where your bliss is, that is where your god dwells.' Then, as St. Augustine advised, 'Love God, and do what you will.' In fact, do not think about God at all, but experience *being* God.

*

So, let there be some light.

Do you see the Light? Do you seek the Light?

Do you have a film in front of your eyes?

Or do you have a film over your eyes?

The Light, said Paracelsus, is the star within us.

Bring forth your own light, however dimly it glows.

Besides aurora borealis and lightning there are: flashlights, hurricane lamps, matches, birthday candles, sparklers, bonfires, and pilot lights.

I Thessalonians 5:5 says; 'Ye are all the children of light.'

Seek, penetrate, magickize!

Radiance is the nature of the Divine.

14

The Brotherhood of Light

So, you want to make a personal film?

You want to bring your visions to life?

Warning: a visionary film is a dangerous quest.

Will you promise to make visible the invisible, express the inexpressible, speak of the unspeakable?

Do you know how to go about it?

Do you know where it will lead you?

*

I can tell you what I know, or think I know, about the making of poetic cinema and the poetry of making cinema. I am not an expert on anything, but I have been a poet clad in movies since childhood and during the past 30 years I have tried to express some of my own visions on film. It's possible that the very next work I attempt may disprove my knowledge. Every new film begins from scratch, from a roll of blank film, as if one knew nothing at all. Another leap in the dark, another jump off a cliff!

So I do not claim to be right about my own pronouncements. As the old sage Lao-Tzu said, no one can be right without also being wrong.

Nor do I have any pretension that I am saying anything new. Wisdoms are clichés; the best ones are great clichés. I set down my own true isms in the form of precept and admonition for the very good reason that they comprise what I repeatedly advise myself.

But if you are a true poet you will pay no attention to good advice. You will make your own mistakes in your own peculiar way and so discover your own wisdom.

*

What is a visionary?

Fellini has replied: 'For me, the only realist is the visionary because he bears witness to his own reality.'

The Initiation: some elementary questions

Has your angel touched you on the shoulder and told you that you must risk all?

Do you believe that you are one of those who must serve the true god of cinema?

Are you willing to live in the dedicated service of the Great Projector?

Are you like the child who cried out on waking, 'Turn on the light! I want to see my dreams!'?

Do you pray to see your own images cast before the world in a beam of light?

*

O the white light! The radiance of the inner light!

O to be a searchlight encircling the seas!

*

Making a film is a more hazardous act than looking at one. For you will create a dream. Whereas dreams themselves are natural events which happen to us. You will create a dream for others to dream and to be dreamed by.

*

Every film is a voyage into the unknown. You set out for great India and arrive at a very small island in the Caribbean. You will need to drag your crew through storms and famine, keep them from mutiny, keep them from suspecting your own doubts. And sometimes, once you have arrived, they will claim the credit and the spoils.

If you don't particularly care for Columbus, would you settle for Vasco da Gama? Magellan? Neil Armstrong? What explorer can cross uncharted seas without a passionate faith in his own vision: the golden images he will discover? This is an attitude toward life, and its ship flies the flag of the poet.

*

I have never begun a film, however well prepared, that did not prove to have a life of its own and lead me to a region where I did not

17

expect to go. What safaris! What narrow escapes! The maps can lead directly to quicksands and the jaws of dragons. Yet sometimes the end of the trail may be quite near King Solomon's mine.

It is not we who play with cinema. The nature of cinema plays with us. Your film knows better than you what form it wants to have, what corners it wants to turn, and what its real meaning is. Let it take you wherever it wants to go. Nietzsche's cry was: Live dangerously! Which is the same thing as: Live poetically!

*

Well, are you ready? Are you willing to be initiated?

It's rather unwise to embark on the high seas without knowing a few of the natural laws of navigation. To have a shipwreck before you have cleared port is both messy and embarrassing. Let's try to get out to the open sea before we urge anyone to Sink or Swim.

Therefore, let's begin with a little catechism.

First of all, do you believe in Light?

Do you seek the Light?

Are you entranced by the Riddle of Lumen?

Does the darkening hall give you an expectation of mysteries to be revealed?

Does the sound of a projector and the flicker of focus leader set your nerves into eager anticipation?

Are you willing to accept Illumination as the true faith?

Do you want to be enlightened?

Do you want to be enlightening?

Do you want to join the Order of the Brothers of Light, founded in 1895 by two French brothers aptly named Lumière?

*

I speak in ecclesiastical terms, not out of frivolity, but because you should understand the seriousness of the way of life you will have to live once you have taken the vows.

If cinema is truly the super art of our century, its iconography unveiled before theater congregations around the world, then it is a calling to be embraced in responsible and solemn terms.

At one and the same time we must ask the best of ourselves and of cinema itself.

*

For the moment, look at cinema as a mystery religion.

Going to the movies is a group ceremony. One enters the darkened place and joins the silent congregation. Like mass, performances begin at set times. You may come and go but you must be quiet, showing proper respect and awe, as in the Meeting House or at Pueblo dances. Up there at the altar space a rite is to be performed, which we are expected to participate in.

Then comes the beam of light out of the shadows: the Projector, the Great Projector up there behind us!

Turn out the little lights so that the big light can penetrate the darkness!

Ah, behold the unreeling of the real reality of practically everything: our dreams, our idiocies and raptures, our nativity, passion and death.

*

Interlude: a short hymn, entitled
     The Secret Name of Cinema is Transformation
   Transform transform
   anything everything—
   stairways into planets
   buttercups into navels
   icebergs into elephants—
      everything
      everywhere
   the old scene renewed by seeing
   the unseen seen anew
      transformed

The Preparation

Before you can be accepted as novice into the Brotherhood of Light, you must first renounce the world and its works. Specifically, the doctrines of the orthodox non-believing fathers: producers, distributors, exhibitors, critics, promoters, hacks, academics, executives, professional moviemen, and all those who condemn acts of vision as a form of heresy. They are terrified by visual phenomena, by personal statement, by the glory of creation, by anything marred by the touch of an artist's own hand. Have no traffic with them. They are the devil's agents who will tell you that you are mistaken, misguided, misbegotten, and a miserable misfit. Don't bother trying to enlighten them. Save your breath and slam the door. They are the enemies of art.

*

'If all men lead mechanical unpoetical lives, this is the real nihilism, the real undoing of the world, to which Dante's Hell is but a fairy story,' said R. H. Blyth in *Zen and Zen Classics*.

Fortunately the Brotherhood of Light is an order wherein the joy of creation reigns and where the agonies of cinema lead to the pleasures it contains.

The Vows

Are you ready and willing to take the Three Vows—the vows of Poverty, Chastity, and Obedience?

Poverty: because you will be forever in debt to the camera store and the laboratory, and will be forever begging from friends and foundations.

Chastity: because you will be wedded to your work and your wildest escapades will be with it.

Obedience: because your life will be in the service of an endlessly demanding tyrant with more heads than a hydra and more legs than a centipede.

And what is the reward for following these vows? Nothing. Nothing but the joy of serving the gods. Nothing but the satisfaction of losing your pants and finding your soul.

The Credo

And now it is time to learn the Credo.

Let us sing in unison:

I believe in the camera, the lens, the filter, the tripod, and the meters of all light.

I believe in the reflector, the quartz lamp, the charges of batteries, and the recording powers of all equipped things.

I believe in the reel, the film stock, the emulsion, and in all the possible pictures of earth and heaven.

I believe in 24 frames per second, the single frame as an atom of time, and all possible metric durations of image.

I believe in the cut, the splice, the A and B roll, the optical printer, and the superimposition of all things.

 I believe in the union of light and darkness, the conjunction of sound and silence, and the projection of these in all times and places.

Furthermore, I believe in the Brothers Lumière, Méliès the Magicker, Our Father Griffith, Sergei the Eisenstein, Carl the Dreyer, Jean the Coctelian, Sts. Von and Von, St. Buster, St. Charlie, and all the other ascended masters and their good works.

And for the community of saints in the modern reformed order of the Far Out Spirit: I believe in St. Deren the Beatified, St. Mekas the Evangelist, St. Brakhage the Redeemer, St. Anger the Demon, St. Baillie the True, St. Peterson the Daedalus, St. Smith the Alchemist, St. Kubelka the Pope, St. Snow the Interminable.

The Pledge

I swear to abstain from all readymade ideas and from all critical assumptions.

I swear to refrain from falling in love with my own footage.

I swear to be precise, ruthless and articulate.

I swear to delight the eye and ear of all creatures.

I swear to attempt the impossible, to exceed myself (no one else), and to venture where no one has ever pushed a button before.

I swear that my aim will always be: to put the right image in the right place at the right time and at the right length.

Here ends the ritual of initiation for the Brothers of Light. The lesson is simple. There are only two commandments on which hang all the loss and the profits: Love thy cinema with all thy heart and with all thy soul and with all thy mind. And love thy fellow filmmaker as thyself.

Now let us pause for our own commercial. 'Wine, music, and cinema are the three great creations of humanity,' said one T'Ian Han, a laureate of Chairman Mao.

Some Rules of the Game

The task remains crashingly simple and endlessly difficult:

1)   2)   3)

Explore! Visualize! Articulate!

Degas said, 'A picture is something which requires as much knavery, trickery, and deceit as the perpetration of a crime.'

Start with light. And delight. Take delight in. Take delight in what is here and what is now. And look at it. And take the light in. And light it. With the delight of light. And the light of delight.

You are a window between the beholder and the beheld.

The secret password is: translucence.

*

Above all you must be a lover. A lover of sights and sounds. Then you must lovingly learn to focus. By which I mean: pay attention, be alert, stretch your senses, think of everything. And you should learn all the rules so that you will know what you have to break.

It is not of camera operation alone that I am speaking. Almost any idiot can learn to do that in a short time. But the more you know about everything besides cinema the better your cinema will be. The more richness of experience you bring to every set-up the better it will set up. The more you know first-hand of painting, poetry, theater, music, color, history, dance, geography, architecture, myth, psychology, magic, and all the other realms of human articulation, the sturdier your film will be.

You may be reeking of talent, but real art comes from knowledge. No work can be greater than the man who made it.

*

So what will your film be about?

It can be about anything. But what do *you* care most about? Stick to your deepest concerns. Don't try to do everything. Debussy found his style by using only those notes that he liked. What are you obsessed by? What haunts your private hours? What do you discover when you go through your own mirror? Tell us, show us! What is going on in the chambers of *your* Hotel des Folies-Dramatiques?

*

Don't waste your time making a film like anyone else's. That's duplication of effort. Besides, it won't be any good. Your business is to make something that neither you nor I have ever seen before. Your business is to make a wonderful new kind of mess in your own way.

If it doesn't fit into any recognizable category for the festivals and the critics, that's too bad. About them. When you have made your own room, room will have to be made for you. Forget about critics. Don't adopt their values or adapt to them. You are not an arbiter of taste. Your business is to be your own man. Your business is to take the risk of your madness. Hello, Columbus.

Excellent strategy: do what you are most afraid of doing. Look what Brakhage did. He has always feared death intensely, it has been a constant threatening imminence for him. So, with the courage that has always made him a trail-blazer, he took his camera tightly in hand and went into the city morgue of Pittsburgh and looked closely and filmed unforgettably the forms of death as they had never been seen before: *The Act Of Seeing With One's Own Eyes.*

Live on the edge! Are you just playing around? What are you saving yourself for? Live as if every day were your last!

*

When I made my first film I thought seriously that it would be the only film I would ever make. *Mother's Day* was not made to please anyone but myself. It was done out of absolute necessity: to discover what my inner haunting looked like. I accepted it as my first and last chance, a one and only shot: I risked everything. All work should be approached that way. Still today every film I make is my 'last.'

*

What does it matter whether *Mother's Day* was influenced by *Blood of a Poet, The Andalusian Dog,* or *Meshes of the Afternoon*? That sort of thing is only a critic's means of putting one in one's place (or some place where he can file you away) so that originality can be discounted.

What if I admitted that my film aesthetically owes much more to my grandmother's family album, to landscapes of De Chirico, music of Stravinsky, and poems of Rilke than it does to anything in film history? Or, what if I acknowledged that the major influence came from the traumas of my childhood that I carried in my heart for 20

27

years before I ever began filmmaking? Godard, in *La Chinoise:* 'Art is not a reflection of reality. It is the reality of a reflection.'

When I made *The Bed* I thought it too was a one and only last picture show. I had not made a film for 13 years and I was prodded into making 'just one more' by Jacques Ledoux of the Belgian Film Archive for his international experimental powwow of 1968. All I did was express how life felt to me in my 50's. *The Bed* has no special style, there isn't a trick in it, it is all straight cuts. I wanted to show as directly as possible my vision of the flowing river of existence and I thought of it as a private communication to an old friend in Brussels. The public success of the film astounded me.

*

Don't think about success, no matter how famous you want to be. Success is out of your hands. That is what other people do with your work. It will happen if it happens, you can't force people to like you. Your business is the achievement: the best you are capable of, however eccentric.

Don't make anything with the desire to impress anybody.

You are more apt to depress them.

Make it to share your delight, to expose your pain.

Make it to please yourself or a friend or a beloved.

Make it to the Glory of God.

Maybe one or two strangers will be illuminated, as you were.

Poetry is an act of love, it asks no rewards.

Remember the caution of Castaneda's Don Juan: 'Does this path have heart?'

Honor your dreams. The gods visit you in your dreams. C. G. Jung carved over his front door: 'The gods are always present, even if uninvited.'

Love your dreams! Expand your dreams!

In Jungian therapy there is a practice called Active Imagination. In this you are urged to take off with a dream you have had, letting it unravel however it wants to: in other words, dreaming awake.

How active is your own imagination? How far do you let it go? For Blake imagination was the star in man. There are many less rewarding pursuits than following a star.

*

If you become familiar with your dreams, you will enter the translucent realm of the archetypes, those potent primal images of mankind. They are much more exciting and abiding than topical events.

Let me quote Jung again: 'He who speaks in primordial images speaks with a thousand voices; he enthralls and overpowers, while at the same time he lifts the idea he is trying to express out of the occasional and the transitory into the realm of the ever-enduring.' Images that grow from our roots to shape the future of mankind are the ones to cherish. The images that you make public become your own mythology and part of the destiny of all men. Dahlberg said it: 'Be primordial or decay!'

'Follow your own Weird.' But this doesn't mean that all you have to do is turn on the camera and express yourself. Just as talking has nothing to do with creating, self-expression has nothing to do with art. 'Anything goes' may be therapy but that is only prelude to the shaping of visions thus discovered. As in painting it is the frame that defines the image, gives shape, selection, point of view, and crystallizes essences.

Nothing is more stimulating to the imagination than working within limitations. Concentrate the magic within the alchemical vessel. Plato's The Container and the Thing Contained.

*

A word about being original. In a word: don't worry about it. A new technique, a new gimmick, is not automatically a new vision. Originality has nothing to do with novelty. The word comes from origin. Thus your original nature is in your roots. As the koan asks, 'What was your original nature before you were conceived?'

Many kinds of clever cinema flourish. Some of it is genuinely innovative, some of it is exhilarating exercise for the eyes. But most of it is what Kubelka calls 'festival kitsch.'

Keep true to your own nature and you will be original enough. Trust your feelings, intuitions, assumptions, attitudes, and follies. Go deep. Don't wrestle with a mouse. Try an angel!

A Zen poem says, 'If you do not get it from yourself, where will you go for it?'

*

If you want to be avant-garde, never do what the avant-garde is doing. By the time everybody knows what's new, it's already old

30

hat. The true scout of the vanguard is already far out of town, exploring a new wilderness. Michelangelo: 'He who follows will never advance.'

The avant-garde task is to deal with what nobody else is attending to. This keeps widening human consciousness and keeps balance in the universe.

As for the form to give your vision, the surest way to look avant-garde is to revitalize an old form. 'There is nothing new but what has been forgotten.' Look at all that Picasso dug up. 'Make it New' was Ezra Pound's motto, and that's what he did with Provencal, Chinese, Anglo-Saxon forms. *The Golden Positions* looks 'new' because I went back to Muybridge.

*

Perhaps the ultimate avant-garde position: to reach the place where you no longer lean on any object, any reference. Or, as with Krishnamurti, 'the stairway without any railing.' Then you might reach the sphere of the innate light, the Mother Light, the light of which all other lights are the children.

Can you go past your dreams to the pure light of dreaming?

*

For the Brothers of Light Cinema is:
    a high form of yoga discipline
    a service of prayer and thanksgiving
    a translucent mystery
    a devotional agony
    a quest for ecstasy

a new creation of the world
a society of explorers
a fellowship of the inner radiance

*

There is a lady in Firbank's novel, *Vainglory*, who shivers ecstatically at the prospect of being memorialized on a stained glass window: 'Oh to be pierced by light!'

Huntsman, What of the Light

Filmmaking is traditionally spoken of as an activity of shooting.

If this is your occupation, aim at being a sharpshooter.

Don't shoot the breeze or shoot the works.

Shoot straight and love the target.

A crackshot is neater than a shot in the dark.

Do you know what kind of a hunter you are?

1) Are you a big game hunter, leading an expedition to a pre-selected veldt where helpers will flush your elephant into the open?

2) Are you a trapper, who builds an artful snare in which to lure his quarry and then waits for the trap to spring?

3) Are you a solitary stalker, who carries his weapon in hand through jungle, desert and mudflat, primed to bag whatever prize he discovers?

4) Are you a trickshot, who wants to dazzle onlookers with daredevil feats of virtuoso marksmanship?

5) Are you a shooting-gallery hunter, who takes rapid-fire potshots at the same duck going by again and again?

6) Are you a trapshooter, who prefers clay pigeons to wild doves?

7) Are you a re-shooter, who likes to shoot over again what has already been shot, whether it's your own game or another's?

8) Are you a star-shooter, shooting into unknown spaces?

9) Are you (is anyone yet) a bodhisattva shooter, aiming to liberate all sentient beings from suffering, ignorance, and fear?

10) Or are you, like most people, just a potshot, more often hit by the target than hitting it?

*

Assuming you are as prepared as you can be, shooting is the easiest part of filmmaking. A hunt can even be a picnic, if you delight in unexpected difficulties. In any case, the worst agonies of cinema pertain to the end of the process more than the beginning: the mixing, matching, labbing, printing. Which could be called: skinning, carving, recycling, and packaging your wild game.

Zen in the Art of Cinema

When logics die
The secret grows through the eye.

– Dylan Thomas

Art is a quest for freedom and Zen is a good way to prepare for the quest. The woods are certainly full of much more misleading alternatives. So many mules palmed off as gazelles! But Zen, after all, is one of the great poetic disciplines of the world.

*

Zen is usually identified as being unidentifiable. One definition (by Taigan Takayama): 'A state of awareness in which one is identified with an object *without any sense of restraint.*' But you can make up your own definition.

Zen means not being enslaved by any point of view. For Zen is not a religion or a philosophy or a theory or a church. It is a poetic way of life. Zen knows the mind is not to be relied upon in crucial matters. (I make my own Zen as I make my own Oz or Christianity. If you swallow bodies of thought whole, you can choke on dogmas.) The true way of discovery is intuition: the poet's archery.

He who knows that flowers are visions
let him enter boldly!

— Gido

*

Nobody can tell you what Zen is, but it's not hard to find out what you do with it.

First of all, you sit. You start your day with sitting and you end your day with sitting. Zenites practice zazen on zafus in a zendo. That's the way you put your mind quietly into your bottom. In solemn circles this is called meditation. Meditation is emptying your mind of all the crap it doesn't need. Meditation is the defecation of the soul.

*

Filmmakers should begin their day with zazen.

Don't be eager to rush out and shoot something.

 Sit awhile first.

Maybe you'll take time to think things through.

Maybe you'll think of something better.

Maybe you'll think the whole thing over and think better of it.

Maybe you won't think of anything. That's all right too.

Maybe the best films are those that don't get made.

40

Not making a film is a very important part of filmmaking.

*

Or, to paraphrase a famous Zen poem:
    Sitting quietly doing nothing
    and the film grows by itself.

Zen is a way of letting things happen. And letting them be.

Zen is the moment in the moment aware of the moment.

And cinema is the greatest collection of moments man has ever collected.

(*High Kukus* is what happened when I sat quietly doing nothing, letting the moment—2.777 minutes of it—reveal itself.)

    I sit at the moon-filled window
    Watching the mountains with my ears.
    Hearing the stream with open eyes . . .
    The most fleeting thought is timeless,
    A single hair's enough to stir the sea.

        — Shutaku, 14th century

*

Zen is another word for Zest. For zip and zap and zing. If you have no appetite for life as it is, and are not excited by the koan of what this here life is about, then Zen is not for you. Try the Holy Rollers instead. For Zen has zest for the whole business from Z to A. Zen really begins with A. And the words of A.

Question: What are the 6 key words of A to be? (in 5 letters each) Answer: *Alive. Awake. Alert. Aware. Agile. Adept.* So, to begin your own Zen, are you alive or are you just going through the motions?

*

According to Mr. Takashi Ikemoto of Yamaguchi City, Zen poetry is characterized by conciseness, rigor, spontaneity, virility, and serenity.

*

The only films worth looking at more than once are those with Zen in them. Even a little Zen helps any movie.

Fritz Lang has no Zen. Busby Berkeley does. Vigo radiates it. Dovzhenko has it in his bones. Japanese films have too little Zen in them and too much John Ford. Buster Keaton is pure Zen. Visconti doesn't know what it is. Bergman has everything but.

*

A Zen dialogue:
    'What is cinema?'
    'The cat is climbing the fence.'
    'But I do not understand.'
    'Ask the fence.'

*

Zen is often zany but it is completely serious.

Zen has no patience with the worthy, the exhaustive, the grand.

Zen is a way of perceiving the serious nonsense of the universe. Hence it is the practice of true poets.

Mozart bubbles with Zen, Wagner hasn't a trace.

Zen giggles with what is most profound. It knows that the irrational is the lifeblood of art.

Mack Sennett had Zen without knowing it. Fellini has Italian Zen.

Above all, Zen has no respect for scriptures, for texts and theories, for the confusing inadequacies of language.

Zen points directly at the thing itself.

When the Zen master pointed at the moon, he said, 'Why are you looking at my finger?'

*

Zen is an art of seeing. It does not follow a script.

Zen says it is not founded on written words but on direct experience. It is outside the established teachings. Hence Zen is truly avant-garde cinema.

Bruce Baillie lives his Zen. Like Gary Snyder.

Brakhage has more Zen than he thinks he has.

Zen has nothing to do with bright ideas. It is seeing the transcendental in the commonplace. Except that there is no commonplace. Every thing is uncommon. To the true poet nothing is trivial. 'If he

43

breathes into anything that was before thought small, it dilates with the grandeur and life of the universe,' said Whitman, who breathed into grass.

Zen is poetry in action. It is the reality one creates out of what already exists. It is the big movie of existence, which is the everyday spectacular, made out of innumerable haiku moments frame by frame. Zen is seeing the light in everything you see.

*

The Zen moment is not the time to be thinking of what you want to 'get' in the scene, or get out of it.

It has nothing to do with any preconceptions or any goals. Joan Miro: 'If you have any notion of where you are going, you will never get anywhere.'

It is the moment to focus your focus on what is there, on what you are really seeing.

A Zen maxim says: 'Don't smoke while peeing.' More politely we could say: 'Don't smoke while looking through the lens.'

This is the moment to focus and center, this is meditation in action, this is the suchness of Is.

> This is It
> This is really It
> This is all there is
> and It's perfect as It is.
> There is nowhere to go but Here
> There is nothing Here but Now.
> There is nothing now but This.

And This is It.
This is really It
This is all there is
and It's perfect as it is.

What you choose to make of It can come after. But first you have to
realize where you are. The fish said to his mother: 'I have heard a lot
about the sea. Please tell me where it is.'

*

Zen is not interested in comparisons, curriculums, concepts, careers.
It wants living experience. Discussing Art is anti-Zen. 'The poetic
imagination,' said Stephen Spender, 'is harmed by absorbing more
intellectual knowledge than it can digest.'

Zen does not make peace with proprieties. It provokes by paradox
and puzzle.

The Zen artist lives as if on the brink of death. The Void of 'black
leader' is always in the offing, ready to engulf the scene.

*

Looking through your lens, are you in the Eternal Now?

Couldn't you use a little Enlightenment?

Wake up then. Wake others up. Be a Zen master.

Hit the dumbbells over the head. With a slapstick.

Or hit the slapper with a dumbbell. But awake!

There is nothing more surprising than right now.

Right now is where you always are anyway.

*

Zen master Ikkyu was asked by a layman: 'Master, will you please write for me some maxims of the highest wisdom?'

Ikkyu immediately took his brush and wrote the word 'Attention.'

'Is that all?' asked the man.

Ikkyu then wrote twice: 'Attention. Attention.'

'Well,' remarked the man, 'I don't see much in that.

Ikkyu then wrote three times: 'Attention. Attention. Attention.'

Irritably, the man demanded: 'What does that word 'Attention' mean anyway?'

Ikkyu answered, gently, 'Attention means attention.'

*

Whatever the price, pay attention. Pay attention whatever price it asks. Otherwise you will pay through the nose for your non-attention. 'Craft is perfected attention,' said Robert Kelly.

*

Do you practice zazen sitting on the naugahyde zafus in the movie theater? Or do you just sit there? What is really going on? Are you paying attention to what is happening or are you too busy forming an opinion? Are you seeing any Light?

*

A blind man was offered a lantern when he was starting home at night. 'I don't need a lantern,' he said, 'light or dark is the same to me.' 'But someone may run into you.' He took the lantern but had not gone very far when someone ran into him. 'Watch where you're going,' said the blind man, 'can't you see my lantern?' 'Your light is out, brother,' came the answer.

*

Zen is anathema to critics because Buddhism insists the universe has nothing to do with good or bad, acceptance or rejection. From the Zen point of view the questions asked by Western thinkers are either frivolous or impertinent. Huang Po said: 'Only when you stop liking and disliking will all be clearly understood.'

*

If you don't have a point of view, how will you ever see the point? Validate your mind. You are what you see. You and the world are one. The world is the creation of your seeing. Live what you see. Live in what you see. Empty your mind of labels, ghouls, and goals!

*

Zen student: If I haven't anything in my mind, what shall I do?

Zen master: Throw it out.

Student: But if I haven't anything, how can I throw it out?

Master: Then carry it out.

*

Bunuel has Catholic Zen. Dreyer has Protestant Zen.

Stravinsky has Russian Zen. Eisenstein almost lost his.

Precise spontaneity is the only way of hitting the target.

When you know how to be where you are and to do what you do, you can take any risk.

Order does not interfere with freedom, as Bach proved.

Bach makes all kinds of freedom live together harmoniously.

*

In his essay *Zen in European Art*, R. H. Blyth lists six qualities which should be present in any picture for it to be truly Zen. These are: naturalness, humor, agedness, latency, sexuality, and joy. Blyth explicates these aspects thus:

Naturalness — simplicity, spontaneity, and inner quietness.

Humor   — paradox, unconventionality, and freedom.

Agedness   — ripeness, timelessness, inevitability.

Latency   — the essence, the unknowable, the potential.

Sexuality   — 'All nature is my bride,' said Thoreau.

Joy   — the exhilaration of reality.

*

The aim of the Zen film student: to see into his own cinema nature and into the cinema nature of Nature. The enlightenment called satori is the lightning result. When you see the Light for sure, you can throw away your light meter.

The Zen filmmaker: Tranquil as a mountain, alert as a cat, natural as a hawk, spontaneous as a monkey, flowing like a river.

Some Koans of Cinema:

Question: Is cinema a means of experiencing satori?

Answer: Satori is the experience of the meaning of cinema.

Question: Is satori a vision of the absolute cinema?

Answer: Satori is a vision of the Absolute Nothingness of cinema.

*

Said the Zen student: 'How does it happen? Now that I am enlightened I am just as miserable as before.'

The Oz of Cinema

Oz is a place all poets should visit once a year.

And before setting forth on any shooting party, filmmakers should stopover in Oz to remind them of what not to forget.

Oz is of a different order of nonsense from Zen.

Zen is where you see what is. Oz is where you see what isn't.

Zen is here, Oz is there. Far out there.

Oz is where there are no parents, no teachers, no preachers, no police, no experts, no press, and no need of them.

Oz is the land of the gleeful and the home of the daft.

Oz is the place to see the innocent Light in the heart.

*

The magic world of Dorothy and the Wizard is an American Mother Goose Utopia.

It is a fountain of youth. Or, more aptly, a fountain of childhood. (Ponce de Leon never found it, so L. Frank Baum created it.)

Like my poet friends who are also devotees of Oz (Duncan, McClure, Brakhage, Jonathan Williams) I make my own Oz just as I make my own Zen.

Where Zen is the land of the zany sage, Oz is the land of the nonsense-loving child. Zen is for the *senex*, Oz is for the *puer*. But they are not really that far apart: the sage enjoys the wisdom of returning to his childhoodness.

*

Oz is run by witches and little girls. Its queen is a 10-year-old named Ozma. No one in Oz can get sick or grow old or die. No one earns a living, puts on weight, or thinks deeply. In short, Oz is everything the U.S. would secretly like to be. The surest way of getting there: go to the very heart of America. That should be Kansas. There get yourself into the cockpit of a cyclone. Off you go! However, the landing fields in Oz are unpredictable. Sensibly there is no airport near the capitol. You are bound to come down in the middle of an adventure, not a predicament.

*

Like the cosmogony of the Navajos, Oz is a mandala composed of four equal countries, north south east and west, that have different colored landscapes. And at its center stands a most American 'jewel in the lotus': a city made entirely of valuable green stuff—emeralds.

*

Oz is where everyone is wealthy and no one is rich.

Oz is how you keep from taking the U.S.A. seriously.

Oz is how you keep the spirit of play alive.

Oz is where you act foolish and end up wise.

Oz is where anything is permitted within the laws of imagination.

Oz is where the Tarot cards are alive and kicking all around you.

Oz is where the unexpected can always be counted on.

Oz is where you take your pants down anywhere.

Oz is where there is no advertising.

Oz is the playground where everything is done for love.

Oz is where there are no media to interfere with your own living moment.

Oz is where you never apologize, never explain.

*

Unless you have some Oz in you, you will go along with President Holdfast and General Apathy. You will believe in doctors, insurance companies, statistics, national defense, pensions, retirement communities, and a thoroughly safe dwindle. You will garner some fringe benefits but miss out on the central Benefit.

If you still have some Oz in you, you will grow younger as you age. You will not only have the serenity of seeing the Light, you will still trip your own fantastic lightly.

Chaplin and Cocteau have Oz in them. But Stroheim doesn't. Harry Smith does and Robert Nelson and Karel Zeman. Brakhage has his special myopic Oz. Méliès has the most far-sighted.

*

Putting Oz in your film is arranging life to suit yourself.

It is a way of prolonging and developing the games of childhood.

It is a way of constructing new and more intricate toys.

It is a way of being loyal to the playfulness of the spirit.

It is a way of fooling around and accidentally discovering a new universe.

*

Cohl and Zecca and Mayakowsky have some Oz.

Does Godard? Does Maya Deren?

Sternberg has more Oz in him than Antonioni.

Murnau had more than he permitted himself.

René Clair once had some.

Keaton has as much Oz as he has Zen.

*

To the serious arbiters of taste any Oz is suspect: gaiety, fantasy, foolishness, and sadness without remorse are plainly marks of a frivolous mind. So they turn gratefully to works of murder, boredom, and despair. And proclaim solemnities to be masterpieces because they are dull.

But in the free world of Oz a child can pluck honey from the paw of a bear.

*

The Oz of cinema is where you can keep your Divine Child uncontaminated by the ignorance of the educated. You can keep his wonder fresh, his irrationality pure, his feeling natural, his invention authentic, his laughter honest. In other words, ready to enter the Kingdom of Heaven.

*

In my own filmography Loony Tom has a certain Oziness. As do Game Little Gladys, the Gardener's Son, Princess Printemps, and The Aging Balletomane. The adults in *Mother's Day* are looking for a lost Oz. Mary Albion, the fat fairy godmother, came pretty directly from Oz or is on her way there; indeed *The Pleasure Garden* is a British annex of Oz. All of *The Bed* takes place in Oz.

*

Film nuts grow on trees in Oz. And all the cameras are magic kits. Ozians relish the unlikely, like true poets. It wouldn't hurt any filmmaker to take a few seminars with the Wizard of Oz and learn a little Hocus Focus. He himself learned a lot from that greatest of wizards, Georges Méliès.

Get some sleight into your hand. Learn the precision of the magician. Prestidigitation is a precious art that can go all the way from the rabbit in the hat to the manifestation of a god. With the proper abracadabra the mystery of mysteries can take place.

*

Some of the people who are at home in Oz: Candide, Klee, Edward Lear, Satie, Tolkien, Robin Hood, Shakespeare, Edith Sitwell, Miro, George McDonald, John Cage, Aleister Crowley, Lewis Carroll, Rousseau, Christian Morgenstern, Ronald Firbank, Edward Hicks, and Anonymous.

*

In recent years some particularly movie characters have moved into Oz. One of them is a dowager from the early days, Queen Trixie of Flix, who dwells in the Hall of the Great Silents. She has gotten fat from long sitting, her eyesight is defective, and she no longer knows one movie from another. But her magic movieola is always going and she loves everything she sees.

One of the muses of cinema sometimes visits Queen Trixie of Flix: a shadowy alluring creature, who has a habit of fading out when you need her most, her name is Oblivia. She makes filmmakers oblivious of everything but film and then leads them and their works into oblivion.

Some of the other muses of cinema are: Lumena, Opia, Ephemera, Insomnia, Nostalgia, and Synchronicita.

Above all of these is, of course, the great goddess CineMa, whom the residents of Cineoz worship religiously. She is a goddess of Time continually weaving for us and through us the fabric of her illusions of the world. All the movies which we imagine we experience in time are generated for us by her dancing web. Endlessly proliferating, she is our mother, our magic and our despair.

*

Long live the land of Oz, whatever name you give it, wherever you find it!

Some Definitions

Kodakery: Pictures are more important than life.

> Example: 'Congratulations, madam. That's a fine looking child you have there.'
> 'Oh, that's nothing. You should see his picture.'

Movieology: Movies are more important than life.

> Example: Among the large crowd not one person was looking at the eclipse of the moon. They were all standing in line at the box office.

Theorology: Theories are more important than movies and life.

> Example: 'When I am showing you a picture,' said the professor, 'it is more important for you to see what I say.'

The Alchemy of Cinema

Concoct an observable eternity

— *Thomas Meyer*

Film has its own peculiar alchemy. This is inaptly called Editing. In truth it is the real opus of cinema.

In the editing laboratory takes place the most crucial and often the most creative part of making a film: the alchemical mystery.

Alchemy is the ancient art of transforming the raw matter of nature into a valuable essence. Sometimes, though rarely, this emerges as precious gold. Usually the alchemist is lucky if he gets quicksilver. But this is an appropriate enough element for the silver screen.

*

Walt Whitman reassures us: 'All truths lie waiting in all things.' The alchemical adept puts his raw material through many changes to rid it of 'impurities.' What he seeks is a solid substance of ineffable value, something 'indescribable and inimitable'—which is how Renoir père described the quality of a great painting.

What can scissors and glue do?

Let us juggle and join and juxtapose!

O what scissors and glue can do!

*

The cinematic alchemist works in the dark of his laboratory for hours, days, months, years, seeking the seemingly impossible task of metamorphosis. With his various paraphernalia he tries to transform the invisible into the visible, or as Redon said, to 'put the logic of the visible at the service of the invisible.'

He searches for that continuously flowing Light which will transform leaden fragments into one glowing jewel. Often enough, alas, his 'original chaos' remains unredeemed.

*

Of the editing process Cocteau said: 'To reorganize chance. That is the basis of our work.'

*

Alchemy is the art of Hermes, the great shape-changer. In the editing laboratory Hermes turns the film into the shape of an authentic illusion.

The Humanist Patrizi proposed to Pope Gregory XIV: 'Let Hermes take the place of Aristotle!'

At my very beginning, with *The Potted Psalm* I learned that no two individuals edit the same footage in any similar way. Every man sees the world arranged to confirm his vision of it. Our joint footage Sidney Peterson abstracted with an emphasis quite different from my own version. Not only were two aesthetics and two mother complexes at variance; we were also two different kinds of alchemists. All alchemists might start from the same raw material, but each would end up with a unique philosopher's stone.

*

Alchemy is seeing into what is not yet visible.

It is a uniting with the incomprehensible that wants to come into being.

It is to discover a microcosm.

It is to release the David hidden in Michelangelo's stone.

It is to unclothe the Inevitable.

'All things are beautiful if you have got them in the right order,' said John Grierson.

*

With the putting together of *Mother's Day* I ventured deep into the alchemical mysteries of film. The completed footage hung for weeks in the bedroom of the Baker Street flat I shared with Kermit Sheets. Night after night the strips of film rustled in the breeze from the open window as I lay awake listening to them, wondering how they would ever fit together, waiting for them to tell me how they would most like to be arranged in time. I had no frame of reference. During the shooting the original plan of the film had turned into something utterly different, something I did not understand but recognized was necessary. Eventually I sat at a dinky Craig viewer hour after hour learning the images, seeking their hidden correspondences, gradually discovering the structure. It was like the unraveling of a secret formula. I was more surprised than anyone by what emerged. And enormously grateful to the Guardian Deities who had made it happen. (They, I find, only like things that are allowed to grow into their true inevitability, they pay no mind to readymades.)

'Everything should be as simple as it is, but not simpler,' said Albert Einstein.

*

The public is only able to see projected films, the poet of cinema has to see the unprojected ones.

I love going to the editing table. It is an altar of mysteries. Dust it off devotedly. Let us consecrate. At any moment a temporal ecstasy may occur.

Is this why professional film editors have the tranquility of priests whereas their missionary brothers out shooting wear a more worried look? Editing is a form of midwifery in which one is confident that some sort of new creature will eventually be born.

Chaplin told Cocteau that after making a film he 'shakes the tree.' One must only keep, he added, what sticks to the branches. People who like puzzles make good editors. An emerging film is a diagram-less crossword, a jigsaw without a known shape. Sometimes it is the trial and error of a labyrinth. As Leonardo da Vinci put it, 'You have to go up a tunnel backwards.'

63

Wagner wrote of Beethoven: 'All the pain of existence is shattered against the immense delight of playing with the power of shaping the incomprehensible.'

*

Requirements of the alchemist: passion, perseverance and prayer. Some of the greatest raptures of cinema occur at the editing bench when an unexpected felicity emerges that is so right and inevitable that one knows one has touched a truth. This is the Eureka moment: the flower has appeared in the stone. A finished film is composed of many such felicities, but they are so absorbed into the structure of the total work that they are taken for granted by the spectator as mere building blocks.

Blake: 'It takes all of creation to make a single flower.'

*

Practically speaking cinema is: putting images together in various musical measures. Editing is the music of cinema, as music is the architecture of time. Editing gives film its form, notation, counterpoint, development, pace, syncopation and style. Such an alchemy should be spared the censorious term of Editing. The art is that of Composing. To edit film is to compose eye music. When you edit do you know what key you are in, what your signature is, what your measures are?

Film as Music

In order to qualify as alchemical adepts, all novices in the Brotherhood of Light are required to study music. (This has nothing to do with listening to records while drinking beer with friends.) Thus you will learn how to observe your film running through the viewer as a musical notation rather than merely a succession of scenes. This will reveal your form, your measure, your long and short notes, your rests, your intervals, your rhythms. You will discover how much the composition of a film relies on its metrics. Thus you can better enjoy what goes on in, for instance, *A Movie* (Conner), *Arnulf Rainer* (Kubelka), *Scenes From Under Childhood* (Brakhage), and *Breathing* (Breer). If you ain't got rhythm, you'll never make it.

Vertov: 'The essence of film is in the interval.'

In music the interval is the fixed relation between two notes. The camera creates fantastic motion in the intervals. In Editing you create even more fantastic motions between the shots. Have you digested your Vertov, not to mention your Eisenstein?

Learn from the best, learn from the masters. If you are a swan, don't hang around ducks. When he went to study modern composition under Schoenberg, John Cage was surprised that the pieces studied were Mozart sonatas.

*

In music any theme can be given whatever tempo and key you want. Similarly you can cut your filmed scene fast or slow; the image will convey its action either way. First, if you like, edit what the pictures are doing. Then recompose the whole thing metrically.

Cinema is a form of opera. Learn your notes. Count your frames. Articulate your rhythms. Phrase your line. Shape your tone. Measure your rests. Practice harmonics. (Is your superimposition a major or a minor chord? A staccato or a resonance?) *Question:* If there are 24 frames per second, how many frames per minute do you have to play with?

65

Furthermore in this medium of durations don't neglect to measure the timeless as well. Great alchemy moves with the primordial rhythms of The Only Dance There Is.

*

Is cinema a Byzantine art?

Putting a film together resembles most of all the art of mosaic. These myriad 'tiles' of image, all the same size and shape in your hand, have to be trimmed, arranged, carefully placed, and glued together to make a total picture. But unlike *The Wedding of Theodora* a film mosaic is never seen in toto. Film is a mosaic on a spool which reveals its total luminosity only after it has been unreeled through Light. It is a mosaic in duration, many pointillist fragments in succession, totally present only when it has disappeared into darkness at The End. Like a symphony.

Hence in composing film we have a craft that might be called *Musaics*. Do you qualify as a musaicist?

Broughton's Musaic Law: Thou shalt glue thy vision note by note until it dance the Light.

Some Mottoes for Editing Room Walls.

> Compose yourself. Then compose.
> Every frame is a moment of Now.
> Take nothing for granted.

By all means try all means.
When in doubt, cut.
(Barbara Linkevitch revised this to rhyme:
When in doubt, cut it out!)
Attain the inevitable.

Some Useful Final Tests

1) Look at your film upside down. This not only gets some blood into your head, it will show you how well your work hangs together. You may also discover that it is really one for the bats.

2) Look at your film with your back. With a mirror, watch your film projected over your left shoulder. This will not only show you what a mirror sees, it will test the sturdiness of your compositions.

3) Look at your film sideways (lying down is the easiest way). Do left and right work as well as up and down?

4) Look at your entire film in reverse. Does Effect stem solidly from Cause? Do Alpha and Omega have good connections? Does the musaic hold together backwards?

*

A film is never finished, it is only abandoned. But if we are wise we are not expecting perfection anyway, since nothing in life is perfect, art included. All we alchemists can hope for: to arrive somewhere close to our original vision. Or, at some more astonishing place than we ever imagined.

'Perfection of thing is threefold; first, according to the constitution of its own being; secondly, in respect of any accidents being added as necessary for its perfect operation; thirdly, perfection consists in the attaining to something else as the end.'

— *Thomas Aquinas*

*

The value of pursuing any art is to live life more ineffably. Or, as Spengler put it, 'we can understand the world only by transcending it.'

My life has prospered when I have remembered to pursue the Essential, the Eternal, and the Ecstatic.

Some Proverbs

Cinema accumulates all the fantasies of mankind.

*

Cinema is the eye with which man sees himself. And it is free to spit in its own eye if it so desires.

*

There is as much bad cinema as there is bad anything else.

*

Film is both a mirror and an ever-expanding eye. It creates what it sees and destroys what it does not see.

*

An image of truth is whatever you believe in.

*

Cinema is almost as perishable an art as cake-making, though not always as tasty.

*

Cinema constantly regurgitates itself. It is a ruminant that loves to chew its old cud.

*

Genius is not having enough talent to do it the way it has been done before.

*

The more original we are, the fewer we communicate with.

*

Cinematic images are only dim reflections of what is really going on in the private visions of mankind.

*

Filmmakers should develop the eyes in the backs of their heads. Those with prehensile tails are even better off.

*

Let your visions grow naturally. It is inadvisable to open a rosebud with a chisel.

*

Question to ask of any film: does it have a sufficiency of the Unknown?

*

Cinema is a lie which makes us realize a truth.

Cinema and the Tao

In some due or undue time comes the time to let your film go. This is the moment of doubt. This is also the moment of Tao. And what does this old Chinese character have to do with filmmaking?

*

Tao is the opposite end of Oz.

Tao is the pleasure garden of the old wise one.

Tao is the realization that one's effortful works are only clouds in the wind.

Tao is what you finally surrender your film to.

Tao is the whole river of cinema flowing down into the murky sea of memory.

Tao is the alternating current that unreels the ever-changing one big movie of practically everything.

*

Cinema is its own Book of Changes. It has, in the end, little to do with works of art as such. It is not an infinite number of separate 'things.' It is a 'sensitive chaos' in duration like the Tao. How can you look at something as a public monument when, while you are looking at it, it is already floating down the river into Elsewhere?

*

If you will allow that your own work is part of the river of time, then it can become an amusement to watch whether it swims or sinks. Besides, you have already outgrown it anyway. The picture you just took of what is happening is not what is happening now.

*

Tao is even harder to define than Zen. Tao is another nonsense syllable which the Chinese use as a name for the way Everything grows, moves, changes, and interacts in its natural spontaneous order.

Zen sees that everything is what it is. Tao moves with everything as it flows.

Zen is the moment of awareness. Tao is letting the moment go.

The Tao of cinema affirms unbroken movement: it never stops, it never turns back, its patterns are real only as they pass. And every observer is himself part of this weblike river. This is the never-ceasing cinema of our light and dark, great and small, dim and bright Yang and Yin.

*

In *The Secret Of The Golden Flower*, that mysterious text of Chinese alchemy, it says that the Tao 'cannot be seen. It is contained

72

in the Light of Heaven. The Light of Heaven cannot be seen. It is contained in the two eyes.' And in the space between the two eyes there is a clairvoyant lens where the Light of Heaven circulates.

*

If you accept the principal of Eternal Change as governing the universe, then to work in a perishable medium like film means that you accept the universe. You can yield and go with it the way a film flows through camera and projector, clicking, bending, warping, scratching, ripping, flickering, burning, shining. Toss your movie into the great river.

What does it matter that you don't know where your films go, who sees them or who doesn't? Either you trust a river, or you don't. Tao means knowing that you don't know, and being happy about it.

*

Certainly you are free to struggle upstream as much as you want to. You can dam your waters. Or divert them to various forms of husbandry. Or drain your swamp and dwell in a desert. But in the end all matters erode, melt, wash away, gravitate to their source and its cycles. This I tried to express in my film for Lao-Tzu, *The Water Circle*, by flowing with a song of renewal and showing the waters as a hand-held dance of Light.

*

I had a dream of the Tao as a fine roomy boat which all Brothers of Light secretly knew about. And when the time came they would all get on board and rock merrily upon the currents as they floated down the filmy river of durational timelessness.

Even the weariest artist winds somewhere safe to see.

*

As Heraclitus might have said, the cinema you stand in is not the cinema you stepped into.

A Taoist is a man whose knowledge and intuition teach him how to harmonize with 'unexpected turbulence' though he lacks any seatbelt to fasten. The ultimate tranquility beyond time and change is the condition of the Taoist immortal. And in their orchid heaven these Immortals drink plum wine, not bitter tea.

Ezra Pound said: 'What thou lovest best remains, the rest is dross.'

*

There is no black and white dualism in Taoist cinema. Its dark is always into its light and its light is always into its dark, for these are not absolutes. They continually flow into one another, overlap, become their opposites. This is symbolized on the revolving reel of the Tai Chi, at the beginning and ending of *Nuptiae*. That symbol is the eternal movie of the Relative Absolute (or Absolute Relative) which might best be expressed by a transcendental double exposure.

Is there a true Taoist film which uses double exposure metaphysically to reveal the play of opposites in every moment of our being? Please try this, someone.

*

Buddhistically speaking, cinema is just a way of filling the Void. Or, trying to. Will the Void ever get completely filled with movies?

Then, will it overflow with old cinematic defecations?

Ask yourself: why do you want to add to this shitpile?

Rilke said, 'A work of art is good if it has grown out of necessity.' Most art works seem to have an instinctive affinity for the non-essential. Stravinsky's customary response at concerts of earnest new music: 'Who needs it?'

*

To be a good revolutionary, the way Stravinsky was, you need also to be a proper conservative. Cherish everything that nourishes the spirit, conserve the sources and resources of the past which can be renewed, and so create rebirths.

Lou Harrison has this alliterative motto: 'Cherish, conserve, consider, create.'

*

Baldinucci wrote of Bernini: 'Preternaturally strong until his last illness, Bernini worked at his sculpture tirelessly, sometimes for seven hours at a time, and always with someone at hand to prevent him from falling off the scaffolding. He worked as if in a trance, and when an assistant urged him to stop and rest, the reply was: "Leave me alone. I am in love." '

*

Love is the ultimate Light. And the Tao is the dance of that Light.

Why not devote your life to being so in love?

Can you think of a more absorbing way to use your time?

Why not take what Keats called The Risk of Happiness?

What do you think you have a 3rd eye for?

Shift your tripod, change your focus: you might see the Light.

You might even *be* the Glory of God.

Then you could be eligible for such an ineffable compliment as the one that a lady paid to the sculpture of David Tolerton:

'Is it real,' she asked, 'or did you make it?'

Seeing the Love Light

Cinema saved me from suicide when I was 32 by revealing to me a wondrous reality: the love between fellow artists.

From *The Potted Psalm* in 1946 to *Erogeny* in 1976 I could not have created anything without sharing love with my collaborators. This is a weakness I take delight in. 'Relations are real, not substances,' said the Buddha. And the more intense the love, the livelier the work. Eros is a true source of the Light.

*

All of my own films have been acts of love. They have been made with love and for love, with the love of others and for those whom I loved. And for the most part the theme of all my work is Love: a call for, a quest for, a fête for.

I meant what I said in *Testament*: I do believe in ecstasy for everyone. There is nothing I would more gladly give to the world, if I could. The ecstatic has been my faith and my adventure.

*

The Brotherhood of Light is, for me, a Brotherhood of Love. There can be no seeing of the light unless there is love to ignite it.

FILMOGRAPHY OF JAMES BROUGHTON

46 - 77

The Potted Psalm	1946
Mother's Day	1948
Adventures of Jimmy	1950
Four in the Afternoon	1951
Loony Tom	1951
The Pleasure Garden	1953
The Bed	1968
Nuptiae	1969
The Golden Positions	1970
This Is It	1971
Dreamwood	1972
High Kukus	1973
Testament	1974
The Water Circle	1975
Erogeny	1976
Together	1976
Windowmobile	1977
Song of the Godbody	1977

BIBLIOGRAPHY OF JAMES BROUGHTON

The Playground	1949
Musical Chairs	1950
An Almanac for Amorists	1955
True & False Unicorn	1957
The Right Playmate	1964
Tidings	1965
Look In Look Out	1968
A Long Undressing	1971
Odes for Odd Occasions	1977
The Androgyne Journal	1977